SHORT TALKS

Anne Carson

Short Talks

with a new afterword by the author
and a new introduction by
Margaret Christakos

BRICK BOOKS

We acknowledge the Canada Council for the Arts and the Ontario
Arts Council for their support of our publishing program.

 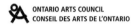

BRICK BOOKS
431 Boler Road, Box 20081
London, Ontario N6K 4G6

www.brickbooks.ca

LIBRARY AND ARCHIVES CANADA CATALOGUING IN PUBLICATION

Carson, Anne, 1950–, author
    Short talks / Anne Carson ; with a new afterword by the author and a new
inroduction by Margaret Christakos. – Brick Books classics first edition, 2015.

(Brick Books classics ; 1)
Poems.
First published: 1992.
ISBN 978-1-77131-342-1 (pbk.)

    I. Christakos, Margaret, writer of supplementary textual content II. Title.
III. Series: Brick Books classics ; 1

PS8555.A7718S5 2015   C811'.54   C2014-905751-2

CONTENTS

INTRODUCTION
BY MARGARET CHRISTAKOS

GLASS, SLAG: SHORT TALK
ON ANNE CARSON'S HEWN FLOWS

■ Ontario, Canada, is not the North, but if you have lived in any part of its upper half for even half a year, you will recognize the soul-hewing problem of sitting in a kitchen and staring out its window at fields "paralyzed with ice" (Anne Carson, "The Glass Essay," *Glass, Irony and God*, 1995). Winter is a weather of mind. Don't get too uppity about your own authority over things, and sort out what to make of boredom as shapeshifter: the silence around thought is part of its sculpture.

April, and still iced everything. I am in my mother's kitchen, in Sudbury. I am here to visit her in eldercare and to think about Anne Carson's *Short Talks*, which presents 45 small taut rectangles of poetic address that each frame a seismic smithering of the human condition. It is immediately obvious, while looking onto the white-out effects of a northern Ontario winter, that the window frame sets Interiorized You in relation to an epic exterior scene. Poetic thought – the boil of the imagination as a response to solitude – is a smelter. Small-town warning flashes: *shit's gonna happen if you think too much.*

That there *is* a speaker is key. *Short Talks* does not frontally expose the aroused scruff of any one self; it is a book of indirect addresses from a chorus of individual voices gesturing personae. Many of the soliloquies are interested in depictions: of the body in visual art and in the illusion of illuminated spaces wherein the body is a studied object or is surgically entered somehow; of historical perspectives on how narrators construct oracular authority; of the body in relation to its domiciles, including wrecked homes and shacks; and of itinerant bodies moving out and on, or transiting from real spaces into sleep. Bodies also appear in vehicles a lot, moving through space and time in cars and trains and television sets. Each poem makes us wake up to a new voice, makes us ask "who is speaking?" Having to resituate among strangers becomes strangely familiar.

My own first copy of *Short Talks* was obtained the year of its original publication, 1992. It is interesting to revisit this series of inventively brief prose poems in light of Carson's subsequent experimental cross-genre body of writing, perhaps best characterized from a present vantage as the gradual importation into her voice-concerned poesis of the fictional scene. *Short Talks* is the moment before Carson moves from portraying lyric mindstage to staging encounters between and among characters. In light of this trajectory *Autobiography of Red*'s Geryon was a revelation. This enactment of character and voice did not only occur in Carson's own poetic fictions; her contemporized translations of Greek tragic plays corrupt those delineations that so often fence off lyric poetry from fiction and drama.

Over the past decades Carson has shown us how to pull very old poetry up through the crust of very new poetry. Her body of writing is renowned for its original, pithy, unruly theatricization of anticipation, desire, insight, terror, shame and resistance. The window frames have exploded; the profuse leakage, onslaught of fire and lava, appears formally alongside something brutally reconstructive in

Carson's present work, all of it engined by the evolution of discernible characters involved in some quotidian, occult, intensely private and profusely choral encounter with perception and mortality.

◊   ◊   ◊

Thinking is related to looking. Although it is late April, stark branches cast weirdly blue and granular shadow-play. So too with grief and anger, I think. In northern Ontario the vision plays tricks, heightening awareness of the distorted figure rendered upon grounds of whitenesses, lucidities and the ever-shifting coloration of shadows – blue, indigo, mauve, royal purple, grey, coal black.

Perhaps because my window is my companion for this re-looking at *Short Talks,* I am moved by Carson's pervasive fascination with perceptions of light, darkness and shadow, along with visual dissemblage and abstractions, as in Seurat's Impressionism – "that place ... [that] lies on the other side of attention" ("... on Chromo-luminarism") – "sleep shapes" ("... on Waterproofing") and "waves" seen as "blue triangles" ("... on the Total Collection"). Like someone wedded to winter panoramas, she draws attention to optical effects of gloss and luminosity, as in the "shiny planes of landscape" ("... on the Rules of Perspective"), and to effects of natural and chemical radiance, as in the phosphorescent fish heart of "... on Shelter." Reflectivity references conditions of spirit – "Terrific lava shone on his soul" ("... on the Youth at Night") – and moral contours of slickened power in, say, "... on Brigitte Bardot," who, "using oil,... will make the slave shine," and in "... on Waterproofing," where Kafka's sister is given a poignantly inadequate "shoeshine" of grease by her non-Jewish husband ("Now they are waterproof, he said.") as she leaves him and her daughters in an effort to protect them after the Nuremburg laws took effect.

Carson has said drawing is far more of an artistic challenge, far more an immersion for her, than is writing. Numerous poems in *Short Talks* reference the visual art image – processes of drawing, figure drawing, rendering perspective, painting, sculpture, printmaking and photography. Writers and European artists – Rembrandt, da Vinci, Van Gogh, Claudel, Braque – are named, amidst themes and scenarios of observing and recording the physical world, following visual lines, having sight impeded or eroded, becoming lost in thought, being blinded or given uncanny sight, being unseen and/or vanishing, becoming banished: familiar postmodern tropes of recognitions and misrecognitions, but there's something material as well – a climate, a bearing of the actual gaze upon place.

Looking out the window, yes, I notice how hard it is, in winter, in April, in Sudbury, to make out the horizon. The far-off white line is a black hole, and vice versa. If you like to think of the distant horizon as a kind of measure of the future toward which you can slouch, well, *you're kinda fucked*. At the buzzy edge that cannot be fixed, the senses mix and contradict, producing a heightened perceptual field, and I notice how Carson's poems, too, render synaesthetic zingers like "eat light," "cries of birds ... like jewels," "light thunders," "scream gazing" and "sun to shadow running down your skull like water."

Other northern sensations rise up as I think of *Short*

Talks: their immersive brevity speaks of corporeal limits, reminding my ear of the short walks that can be taken in very cold places. Each step breaks crisp snow, which talks back to the walker, sonic; also, human skin quickly becomes crisp. Terse elocution is demanded of the body, and on a sunny day the exhilarating snow dazzles vision to the point of a blinding. These ideas move through the brain: *be quick, soak it in, beware the black hole that ice light brings.* Incandescence, how glass is made, first flame, and cooling.

◊   ◊   ◊

In some ways it seems hard to connect *Short Talks* to her most radical current work, *Red Doc>*, but "The Glass Essay," written during the same period, is a precursor to the "scenography" of Carson's future novels, translations and intergenre renderings. In a great *Paris Review* interview with Will Aitken in 2002, Carson describes this writing as failing in some way, but I wonder if it's just that the work is early, and lyric-confessional in modality. The I in "The Glass Essay" is a woman writer who has returned home to visit her mother. She is in her mother's house. Her lover, "Law," has left her. She is deeply interested in Emily Brontë, a writing woman whose life seemed not on its narrative record to include sex with (living) men (God remains a possibility). The concept that sexual energies exceed the present permeates; these are bolts from underground, over-land, a virtual blaze to erase solitude's shape. The Brontë sisters appear in *Short Talks* as well, but as an ensemble, with Emily's early death an imprint upon the other two.

Carson's Emily Brontë, who asserts that "there are many

ways of being held prisoner," is easy to transplant to a frozen lake in northern Ontario because Carson puts her in dangerous discourse with the particularities of a landscape I recognize – "bare blue trees and bleached wooden sky of April / carve into me with knives of light." "Glass" depicts Emily as "Unsociable / even at home," a "raw little soul" "caught by no one," who wrote of "prisons, / vaults, cages, bars, curbs, bits, bolts, fetters, / locked windows, narrow frames, aching walls."

This portrait compels me to read across the texts, for *Short Talks* is a collection also invested in the constraining framework, in concentrated speech acts parsed from historical and temporal expanses, and in the arrangement of fragmentary thought. So preoccupying is the wide aggregate of cultural references across the book that it's easy to miss the vocal exchanges of ordinary families who have trouble talking openly. I start to sense an indirect small-town atmosphere when it comes to conversation: *Don't be too full of yourself.* Embodiment is interestingly at stake. The "Tell me" and "Trust me" instructions near *Short Talks*' end are not, even for a second, simple.

Small-town. In the Aitken interview, Carson explains that her childhood was moved from Ontario town to town because her father was a branch banker. Born on the summer solstice (a Gemini on Cancer's cusp, really!), her teenaged years and much-touted exposure to Latin and Greek occurred in Port Hope, in Toronto's corona. But earlier, apparently, she lived farther from the metropolis, in Stoney Point (near Windsor, wintry enough, a small town with a lumbering history and more recent Indigenous reclamation activism) and in Timmins (true blue-ribbon Winter – in the winter of 1958–59, for example, snow fell from October 1 to May 17). I went to Timmins once, on a winter school trip. Jesus. There is a town in north Ontario, indeed.

In addition to specializing in epic winters, mid-20th century Timmins was a gold-mining global centre, elemental, undertunnelled, the earth upheaved and constantly milled for capital, an industrially mulched moorscape where the pouring of molten slag was a form of cinema. How then to *not* re-read this line in "... on Orchids"?: "We live by tunnelling for we are people buried alive." Out the front window I detect the slag-humped horizon of my hometown's basin where, when I was a kid, spark-orange dregs from the refining of earth's nickelguts were nightly poured. A nice outing was you'd get an ice cream and go in pyjamas in the station wagon and see something pretty close to volcanic spill. Forget the ashes to ashes business. Over and over you imagined your cold body eaten by sticky fire. Could there be a worse, or a better, death?

Though Carson deploys a disciplined code, the poet is neither blithe nor intact; *Short Talks* contains an almost endless buried resource of tectonic emotion. This buried rage is closer to the surface in "The Glass Essay," the narrator's dreams of volcanoes are anger, "blue and black and red blasting the crater open." The "Glass" narrator has short talks with herself: "I want to be beautiful again, she whispers." "I want to curse the false friend who said I love you forever. Slam." She refers to a vindictive anger that permeates Emily's poetry, and wonders how with her untouched life Emily came "to lose faith in humans." She claims to know why her own anger grips her, that the betrayal of losing love from Law is the "stunning," infectious moment.

In *Short Talks,* many of the poems suggest the solitude of the thinker, sometimes pointing to absent-minded physical attendance or proxy ("... on Disappointments in Music"). "Glass" more openly suggests that Emily Brontë's poetry offers a short talk about loneliness: "The heart is dead since infancy. / Unwept for let the body go." The narrator extrapolates, "[o]ne way to put off loneliness is to interpose God." She suggests that Brontë's loneliness is in a kind of perennial conversation with Thou, her God, and is in this way accompanied. The narrator slips into an anecdote about being age eleven in the car backseat – classic 1960s nuclear-family scene – attempting to decode a short talk going on between the heads of her parents, then overhearing her mother on the phone. "Well a woman would be just as happy with a kiss on the cheek / most of the time but YOU KNOW MEN."

The "Glass" narrator articulates both enmeshment in care for aging parents and distinct critical distance from them. An ill father is visited in chronic care. Going home, being at home, involves short talks, a mother's admonishments about closing night curtains, a father with dementia no longer recognizing his daughter and rambling on the phone. "He is addressing strenuous remarks to someone in the air between us. / He uses a language known only to himself, / ... for more than three years now."

Time exerts a double stream of change upon the parent: "[S]ince he came to hospital his body has shrunk to the merest bone house – / except the hands. The hands keep growing." Intensely similar hands ghost Carson's "Short Talk on Sleep Stones." Many of the book's other predicaments relate to troubled speech: how "dishonour ... causes ... vocal chords to swell" ("... on Defloration"); the suppression of voice, as in Kafka instructed not to speak in a sanitorium, leaving "glass sentences all over the floor" ("... on Rectification"); as well as resistant speaking in code, and self-deception, sinning or cheating, and forms of punishment including the ouster. There is also a wrestle against fate, a bitterness about upheavals of luck, a confrontation of life's wreckage where past and present dissolve and swap places ("... on Where to Travel") and a survival of near-death, as in the few "'remaining trout'" that "spent the winter in deep pools" ("... on Trout"). Visiting my own mother, whose post-stroke paraphasia has vastly scrambled her speech, I sense the rage that can fuel poetry's erudite castings of the personal.

◊   ◊   ◊

Although Carson's widely known essay "The Gender of Sound," included in *Glass, Irony and God*, studies the social stifling of women's sexual pleasure, volcanic grief and sintering rage, *Short Talks* arrive freshly at their podium without much body at all, let alone gendered embodiment. Unlike the "Glass Essay"'s romanticist pantomime, which ends up portraying grief, rage and humiliation as a series of visual "Nudes" suffering physical horrors, Carson makes a leap in *Short Talks* beyond the limits of body, swerving instead toward the voice's uncannily mobile flux. Without the contours of skin and flesh, the self remains fluent, loaded with perpetuity.

The volume you are holding in your hand – *Short Talks* – is, I propose, a unique form of slag-like poetic address that arises from the full formative force of Carson's young embodiment of a northern Ontario mining-town winter of mind. It is fascinating to read across texts that Carson wrote contemporaneously earlier in her career, to probe the reputation of a writer who has increasingly been called "inscrutable," and to explore literary extraction processes that include her intense formation in the geophysical and metavisual world. As telescoped in *Short Talks*, Carson's body of work continues to mine fields and substrata of surgical, incandescent imagery that mirrors industrial-Ontario origins. And by chance or design – with Classical wryness – the entire world's *most* ancient water was found, in 2013, gushing from deep-mining boreholes 2.4 miles beneath Timmins.

MARGARET CHRISTAKOS · 2014, Sudbury

SHORT TALKS

Early one morning words were missing.
Before that, words were not. Facts were,
faces were. In a good story, Aristotle tells
us, everything that happens is pushed by
something else. One day someone noticed
there were stars but no words, why? I've
asked a lot of people, I think it is a good
question. Three old women were bending
in the fields. What use is it to question us?
they said. Well it shortly became clear that
they knew everything there is to know about
the snowy fields and the blue-green shoots
and the plant called "audacity," which poets
mistake for violets. I began to copy out ev-
erything that was said. The marks construct
an instant of nature gradually, without the
boredom of a story. I emphasize this. I will
do anything to avoid boredom. It is the task
of a lifetime. You can never know enough,
never work enough, never use the infinitives
and participles oddly enough, never impede
the movement harshly enough, never leave
the mind quickly enough.

In fifty-three fascicles I copied out every-
thing that was said, things vast distances
apart. I read the fascicles each day at the
same time, until yesterday men came and

took up the fascicles. Put them in a crate. Locked it. Then together we viewed the landscape. Their instructions were clear, I am to imitate a mirror like that of water (but water is not a mirror and it is dangerous to think so). In fact I was the whole time waiting for them to leave so I could begin filling in the parts I missed. So I am left with three fascicles (which I hid). I have to be careful what I set down. Aristotle talks about probability and necessity, but what good is a marvel, what good is a story that does not contain poison dragons. Well you can never work enough.

With small cuts Cro-Magnon man record-
ed the moon's phases on the handles of
his tools, thinking about her as he worked.
Animals. Horizon. Face in a pan of water.
In every story I tell comes a point where I
can see no further. I hate that point. It is why
they call storytellers blind – a taunt.

Soon I hope to live in a totally rubber house.
Think how quickly I will be able to get from
room to room! One good bounce and you're
there. I have a friend whose hands were
melted off by a firebomb during the war.
Now, once again, he will learn to pass the
bread at the dinner table. Learning is life. I
hope to invite him over this evening in fact.
Learning is the same colour as life. He says
things like that.

Sunlight slows down Europeans. Look at all those spellbound people in Seurat. Look at Monsieur, sitting deeply. Where does a European go when he is "lost in thought?" Seurat – the old dazzler – has painted that place. It lies on the other side of attention, a long lazy boat ride from here. It is a Sunday rather than a Saturday afternoon there. Seurat has made this clear by a special method. *Ma méthode,* he called it, rather testily, when we asked him. He caught us hurrying through the chill green shadows like adulterers. The river was opening and closing its stone lips. The river was pressing Seurat to its lips.

The question of geisha and sex has always been complex. Some do, some don't. In fact, as you know, the first geisha were men (jesters and drummers). Their risky patter made the guests laugh. But by 1780 "geisha" meant woman and the glamorous business of the tea houses had been brought under government control. Some geisha were artists and called themselves "white." Others with nicknames like "cat" or "tumbler" set up shacks every night on the wide riverbed, to vanish by dawn. The important thing was, someone to yearn for. Whether the quilt was long, or the night was too long, or you were given this place to sleep or that place to sleep, someone to wait for until she is coming along and the grass is stirring, a tomato in her palm.

SHORT TALK ON
GERTRUDE STEIN ABOUT 9:30 P.M.

How curious. I had no idea! Today has
ended.

He would encourage me to move about the studio. Would not give me a pose. Drew without looking at the paper. Drew on the floor. Follow the lines, he would say, watch the surroundings. A thin arm makes a face sadder. Describing shadows he grew small, rascally.

Here is one thing you can do if you have no house. Wear several hats – maybe three, four. In the event of rain or snow, remove the one(s) that get(s) wet. Secondly, to be a householder is a matter of rituals. Rituals function chiefly to differentiate horizontal from vertical. To begin the day in your house is to "get up." At night you will "lie down." When old Tio Pedro comes over for tea you will "speak up," for these days his hearing is "on the decline." If his wife is with him you will be sure to have "cleaned up" the kitchen and parlour, so as not to "fall" in her opinion. Watching the two of them, as they sit side by side on the couch smoking one cigarette, you feel your "heart lift." These patterns of up and down can be imitated, outside the house, in vertical and horizontal designs upon the clothing. The lines are not hard to make. Hats do not need to be so decorated for they will "pile up" on your head, in and of themselves, *qua* hats, if you have understood my original instruction.

Prokofiev was ill and could not attend the performance of his First Piano Sonata played by somebody else. He listened to it on the telephone.

I went travelling to a wreck of a place. There were three gates standing ajar and a fence that broke off. It was not the wreck of anything else in particular. A place came there and crashed. After that it remained the wreck of a place. Light fell on it.

It is the names Northland Sante Fe Nickle
Plate Line Delta Jump Dayliner Heartland
Favourite Taj Express it is the long lit win-
dows the plush seats the smokers the sleep-
ing cars the platform questions the French
woman watching me from across the aisle
you never know the little lights that snap
on overhead the noctilucal areas the cheek-
wary page turning of course I have a loyal
one at home it is the blue trainyards the
red switch lights the unopened chocolate
bar the curious rumpled little ankle socks
speeding up to 130 kilometres per hour black
trees crowding by bridges racketing past the
reading glasses make her look like Racine
or Baudelaire *je ne sais plus lequel* stuffing
their shadows into her mouth *qui sait même
qui sait.*

In haiku, according to Kawabata, there are various sorts of expressions about trout. 'Autumn trout' and 'rusty trout' and 'descending trout' are some that he names. 'Autumn trout' and 'rusty trout' are trout that have laid their eggs. Worn out, completely exhausted, they are going down to the sea. Of course, he adds, there were occasionally trout that spent the winter in deep pools. These were called 'remaining trout.'

I see him there on a night like this but cool,
the moon blowing through black streets.
He sups and walks back to his room. The
radio is on the floor. Its luminous green
dial blares softly. He sits down at the table;
people in exile write so many letters. Now
Ovid is weeping. Each night about this time
he puts on sadness like a garment and goes
on writing. In his spare time he is teaching
himself the local language (Getic) in order
to compose in it an epic poem no one will
ever read.

She cannot quite hear what the doctor is saying it is a large grey cheerful woman its language is boomings beckonings boulders boasts boomerangs bowler hats. Brother? Tell me about your brother? From the tip of its pencil *what does it eat, light?* shriller than a rat's scream slices her backwall into *what does it* jump blue and grabs at them cuts herself off at the root now adrift on that wayland membrane where *what does* wander yondering all those blades of asunder her *what* flying off in conversation all her life and *eat* kept *eat* going let's say they're at large somewhere say Central Park doing *eat eat eat* who knows what damage *eat light?*

We pride ourselves on being civilized people. Yet what if the names for things were utterly different? Italy, for example. I have a friend named Andreas, an Italian. He has lived in Argentina as well as in England, and also Costa Rica for some time. Everywhere he lives, he invites people over for supper. It is a lot of work. Artichoke pasta. Peaches. His deep smile never fades. What if the proper name for Italy turns out to be Brzoy? – will Andreas continue to travel the world like the wandering moon with her borrowed light? I fear we failed to understand what he was saying or his reasons. What if every time he said *cities* he meant *delusion*, for example?

The actions of life are not so many. To go in, to go, to go in secret, to cross the Bridge of Sighs. And when you dishonoured me I saw that dishonour is an action. It happened in Venice, it causes the vocal chords to swell. I went booming through Venice, under and over the bridges, but you were gone. Later that day I telephoned your brother. What's wrong with your voice? he said.

Major things are wind, evil, a good fighting horse, prepositions, inexhaustible love, the way people choose their king. Minor things include dirt, the names of schools of philosophy, mood and not having a mood, the correct time. There are more major things than minor things overall, yet there are more minor things than I have written here, but it is disheartening to list them. When I think of you reading this I do not want you to be taken captive, separated by a wire mesh lined with glass from your life itself, like some Elektra.

SHORT TALK ON
THE RULES OF PERSPECTIVE

A bad trick. Mistake. Dishonesty. These are the view of Braque. Why? Braque rejected perspective. Why? Someone who spends his life drawing profiles will end up believing that man has one eye, Braque felt. Braque wanted to take full possession of objects. He has said as much in published interviews. Watching the small shiny planes of the landscape recede out of his grasp filled Braque with loss so he smashed them. *Nature morte,* said Braque.

Day after day I think of you as soon as I wake
up. Someone has put cries of birds on the
air like jewels.

Brigitte Bardot is on the prowl. What does she want, a slave? to satisfy her hungers and make beautiful photographs. Whose slave is it? She does not care, she never blames herself. Using oil she will make the slave shine. Perfect. *La folie,* she will think to herself.

Kafka liked to have his watch an hour and a half fast. Felice kept setting it right. Nonetheless for five years they almost married. He made a list of arguments for and against marriage, including inability to bear the assault of his own life (for) and the sight of the nightshirts laid out on his parents' beds at 10:30 (against). Hemorrhage saved him. When advised not to speak by doctors in the sanatorium, he left glass sentences all over the floor. Felice, says one of them, had too much nakedness left in her.

The reason I drink is to understand the yellow sky the great yellow sky, said Van Gogh. When he looked at the world he saw the nails that attach colours to things and he saw that the nails were in pain.

Camille Claudel lived the last thirty years of her life in an asylum, wondering why, writing letters to her brother the poet, who had signed the papers. Come visit me, she says. Remember I am living here with madwomen, days are long. She did not smoke or stroll. She refused to sculpt. Although they gave her sleep stones – marble and granite and porphyry – she broke them, then collected the pieces and buried these outside the walls at night. Night was when her hands grew, huger and huger until in the photograph they are like two parts of someone else loaded onto her knees.

SHORT TALK ON
WALKING BACKWARDS

My mother forbad us to walk backwards.
That is how the dead walk, she would say.
Where did she get this idea? Perhaps from
a bad translation. The dead, after all, do not
walk backwards but they do walk behind us.
They have no lungs and cannot call out but
would love for us to turn around. They are
victims of love, many of them.

Franz Kafka was Jewish. He had a sister, Ottla, Jewish. Ottla married a jurist, Josef David, not Jewish. When the Nuremburg laws were introduced to Bohemia-Moravia in 1942, quiet Ottla suggested to Josef David that they divorce. He at first refused. She spoke about sleep shapes and property and their two daughters and a rational approach. She did not mention, because she did not yet know the word, Auschwitz, where she would die in October 1943. After putting the apartment in order she packed a rucksack and was given a good shoeshine by Josef David. He applied a coat of grease. Now they are waterproof, he said.

Every day he poured his question into her, as you pour water from one vessel into another, and it poured back. Don't tell me he was painting his mother, lust, etc. There is a moment when the water is not in one vessel nor in the other – what a thirst it was, and he supposed that when the canvas became completely empty he would stop. But women are strong. She knew vessels, she knew water, she knew mortal thirst.

What is the difference between light and lighting? There is an etching called *The Three Crosses* by Rembrandt. It is a picture of the earth and the sky and Calvary. A moment rains down on them, the plate grows darker. Darker. Rembrandt wakens you just in time to see matter stumble out of its forms.

Did you see her mother on television? She said plain, burned things. She said I thought it an excellent poem but it hurt me. She did not say jungle fear. She did not say jungle hatred wild jungle weeping chop it back chop it. She said self-government she said end of the road. She did not say humming in the middle of the air what you came for chop.

Some fathers hate to read but love to take the family on trips. Some children hate trips but love to read. Funny how often these find themselves passengers in the same automobile. I glimpsed the stupendous clearcut shoulders of the Rockies from between paragraphs of *Madame Bovary.* Cloud shadows roved languidly across her huge rock throat, traced her fir flanks. Since those days I do not look at hair on female flesh without thinking, Deciduous?

It was blacker than olives the night I left. As I ran past the palaces, oddly joyful, it began to rain. What a notion it is, after all – these small shapes! I would get lost counting them. Who first thought of it? How did he describe it to the others? Out on the sea it is raining too. It beats on no one.

A mythical animal, the vicuña fares well in the volcanic regions of northern Peru. Light thunders down on it, like Milton at his daughters. Hear that? – they are counting under their breath. When you take up your axe, listen. Hoofbeats. Wind.

From childhood he dreamed of being able to keep with him all the objects in the world lined up on his shelves and bookcases. He denied lack, oblivion or even the likelihood of a missing piece. Order streamed from Noah in blue triangles and as the pure fury of his classifications rose around him, engulfing his life they came to be called waves by others, who drowned, a world of them.

Miss Brontë & Miss Emily & Miss Anne
used to put away their sewing after prayers,
and walk all three one after the other round
the table in the parlour till nearly eleven
o'clock. Miss Emily walked as long as she
could, and when she died Miss Anne & Miss
Brontë took it up – and now my heart aches
to hear Miss Brontë walking, walking on
alone.

Are you going to put that chair back where it belongs or just leave it there looking like a uterus? (Our balcony is a breezy June balcony.) Are you going to let your face distorted by warring desires pour down on us all through the meal or tidy yourself so we can at least enjoy our dessert? (We weight down the corners of everything on the table with little solid silver laws.) Are you going to nick your throat open on those woodpecker scalps as you do every Sunday night or just sit quietly while Laetitia plays her clarinet for us? (My father, who smokes a brand of cigar called *Dimanche Éternel,* uses them as ashtrays.)

The youth at night would have himself driven around the scream. It lay in the middle of the city gazing back at him with its heat and rosepools of flesh. Terrific lava shone on his soul. He would ride and stare.

A winter so cold that, walking on the Breestraat and you passed from sun to shadow you could feel the difference run down your skull like water. It was the hunger winter of 1656 when Black Jan took up with a whore named Elsje Ottje and for a time they prospered. But one icy January day Black Jan was observed robbing a cloth merchant's house. He ran, fell, knifed a man and was hanged on the twenty-seventh of January. How he fared then is no doubt known to you: the cold weather permitted Dr. Deyman to turn the true eye of medicine on Black Jan for three days. One wonders if Elsje ever saw Rembrandt's painting, which shows her love thief in violent frontal foreshortening, so that his pure soles seem almost to touch the chopped open cerebrum. Cut and cut deep to find the source of the problem, Dr. Deyman is saying, as he parts the brain to either side like hair. Sadness comes groping out of it.

We live by tunnelling for we are people buried alive. To me, the tunnels you make will seem strangely aimless, uprooted orchids. But the fragrance is undying. A Little Boy has run away from Amherst a few Days ago, writes Emily Dickinson in a letter of 1883, and when asked where he was going replied, Vermont or Asia.

Je haïs ces brigands! said an aristocrat named M-ski one day in Omsk as he strode past Dostoevski with flashing eyes. Dostoevski went in and lay down, hands behind his head.

Seized by a sudden truth I started up at
4 a.m. The word *grip* pronounced "gripe"
is applied only to towns, cities and habita-
tions; the word *gripe* pronounced "grip" can
be used of human beings. In my dream I
saw the two parts of this truth connected by
a three-mile long rope of women's hair. And
just at that moment all the questions of male
and female soul murder, which were to be
answered as soon as I pulled on the rope,
broke away and fell in a chunk back down
the rocky chasm where I had been asleep.
We are the half and half again, we are the
language stump.

SHORT TALK ON HÖLDERLIN'S WORLD NIGHT WOUND

King Oedipus may have had an eye too many, said Hölderlin and kept climbing. Above the tree line is as blank as the inside of a wrist. Rock stays. Names stay. Names fell on him, hissing.

Well you know I wonder, it could be love
running towards my life with its arms up
yelling *let's buy it what a bargain!*

My task is to carry secret burdens for the
world. People watch curiously. Yesterday
morning at sunrise for example, you could
have seen me on the breakwall carrying
gauze. I also carry untimely ideas and sins
in general or any faulty action that has been
lowered together with you into this hour.
Trust me. The trotting animal can restore
red hearts to red.

Beauty makes me hopeless. I don't care why anymore I just want to get away. When I look at the city of Paris I long to wrap my legs around it. When I watch you dancing there is a heartless immensity like a sail- or in a dead calm sea. Desires as round as peaches bloom in me all night, I no longer gather what falls.

He arose laden with doubt as to how he should begin. He looked back at the bed where the grindstone lay. He looked out at the world, the most famous experimental prison of its time. Beyond the torture stakes he could see, nothing. Yet he could see.

You can write on a wall with a fish heart, it's because of the phosphorous. They eat it. There are shacks like that down along the river. I am writing this to be as wrong as possible to you. Replace the door when you leave, it says. Now you tell me how wrong that is, how long it glows. Tell me.

I want to know who you are. People talk about a voice calling in the wilderness. All through the Old Testament a voice, which is not the voice of God but which knows what is on God's mind, is crying out. While I am waiting, you could do me a favour. Who are you?

AUTHOR'S AFTERWORD

An afterword should leave the skin quickly, like an alcohol rub. Here is an example, from Emily Tennyson's grandmother, her complete diary entry for the day of her wedding, May 20, 1765:

Finished *Antigone,* married Bishop.

ANNE CARSON was born in Canada and teaches ancient Greek for a living. ⁊ MARGARET CHRISTAKOS is the author of nine books of poetry, including *Excessive Love Prostheses, Sooner, Welling* and *Multitudes*. She has taught part-time with creative writing programs including the University of Guelph MFA, OCAD University and University of Toronto School of Continuing Studies, where she designed and facilitated *Influency: A Toronto Poetry Salon*.

Books in the Brick Books Classics
series are designed by Robert
Bringhurst. ¶ The text face in
this volume is Scala, designed in
Utrecht in 1989 by Martin Majoor.
¶ The type on the cover is Palatino
Sans, designed 1973–2006 by
Hermann Zapf. The bricks were
made in the early 20th century
from Vancouver Island clay and
aged in the coastal rainforest.

BRICK BOOKS CLASSICS